Our New Baby in the NICU

A Special Book for the Big Brothers and Sisters

Words Worth Repeating

Written and Illustrated by Laura Camerona, CCLS

Dedicated to all of the women and men who give so much themselves to take care of these sweet babies and their families. I have learned so much from so many of you.

A special thank you to the NICU staff that helped edit and advise.

ISBN Paperback 978-1-7367884-8-6

Published by

Words Worth Repeating

www.wordsworthrepeating.com

Tips for Supporting a Sibling during a NICU Stay

-Ask staff if your NICU has a Child Life Specialist. Consult this hospital professional for free advice and support for the baby's sibling.

-If allowed and appropriate, bring the big brother or sister to visit the baby in the NICU. Prepare the brother or sister before they go into the NICU. Reading this book and talking about what they will see is one way to prepare a child. The first time the child visits, it is important to have another adult with you. This will give you some flexibility, if your child is ready to go, and you need to stay.

-For younger children, have a baby doll at home that allows your child to play through what they are experiencing. When you have time, consider playing "hospital" with your child. Play is how children learn.

-Take a photo of the big brother or sister to the NICU and attach it to the baby's crib. Show the big brother/sister a picture of their new baby next to the photo.

-Don't make any promises. Babies and healthcare are hard to predict. Even if a nurse or doctor tells you that you will probably "go home tomorrow", prepare your child with "our baby MIGHT come home tomorrow". Babies can have a spell, lowered heart rate, or lab result that keeps them in the NICU for a few more days.

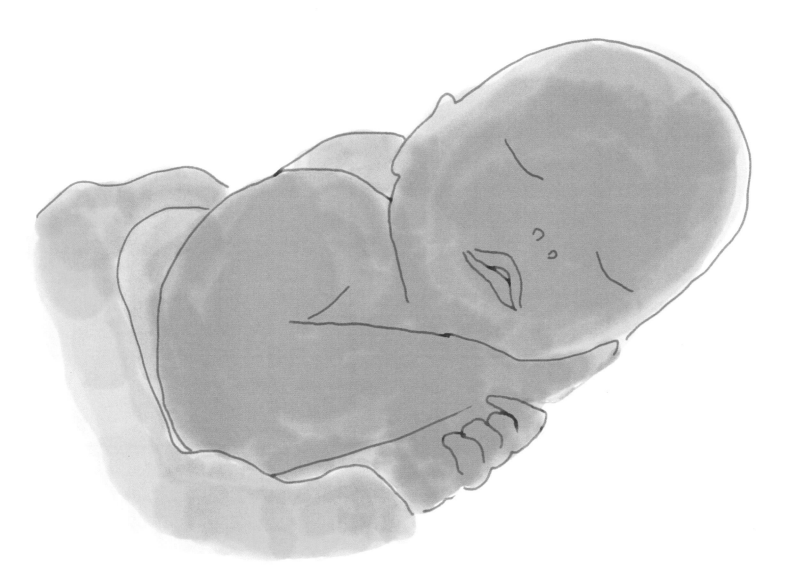

There is a new baby in our family. Our new baby's name is
_____. I am the baby's new big
_____ (brother/sister)!

Right now, our new baby has to stay at the hospital. Our baby is in a special part of the hospital called the NICU.

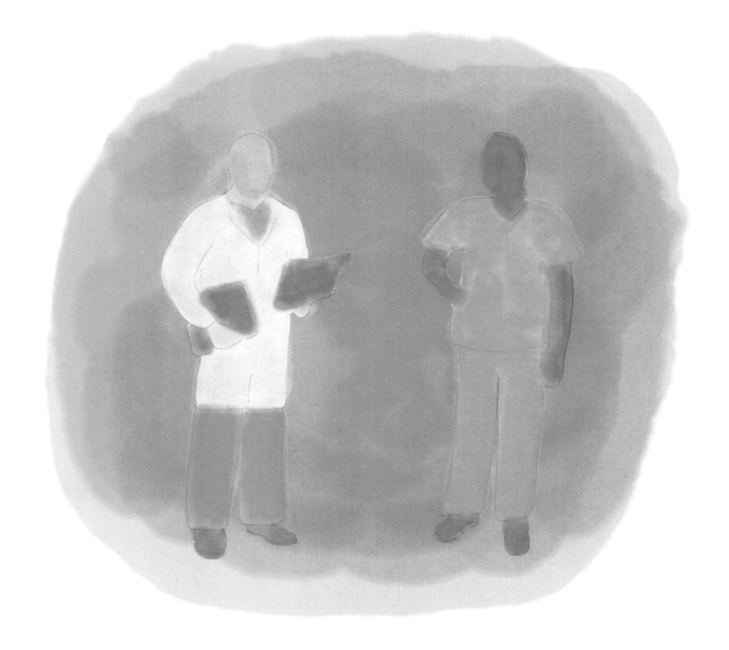

The doctors, nurses, and other people who work in the NICU have taken care of a lot of babies. They will take very good care of our baby!

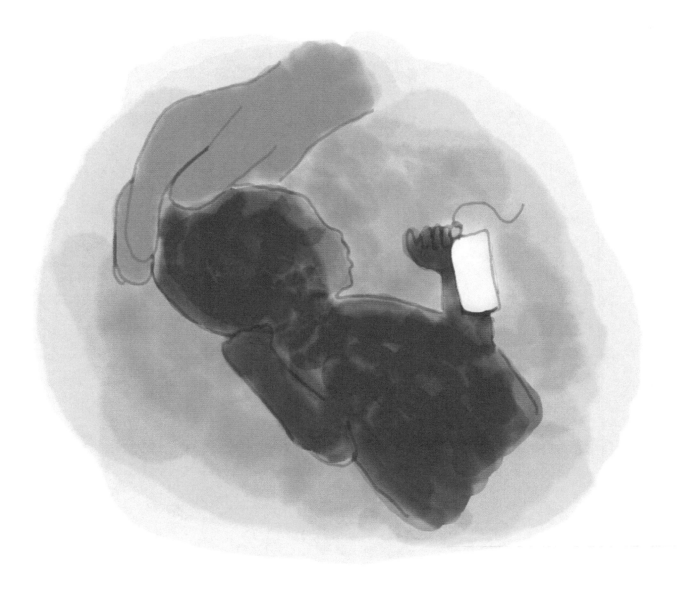

Our baby is not the only baby in the NICU. Babies that need extra help before they are ready to go home stay in the NICU.

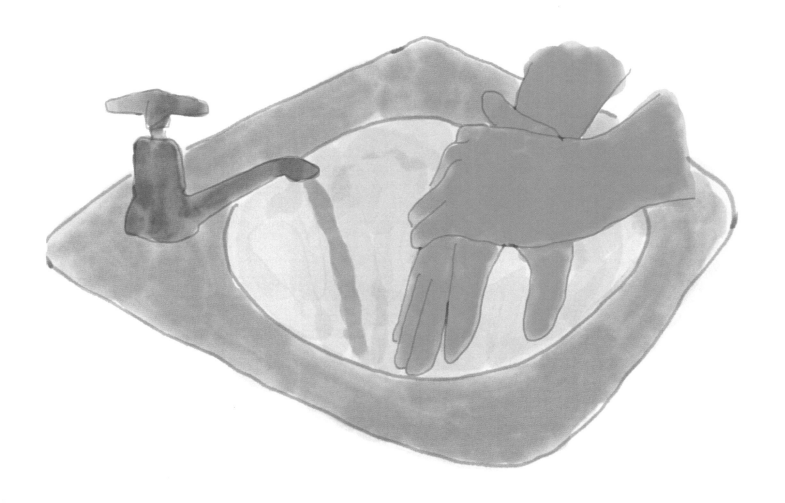

It is important to keep germs away from the babies in the NICU.
Everyone in the NICU washes their hands a lot. People can not visit
the NICU if they are sick.

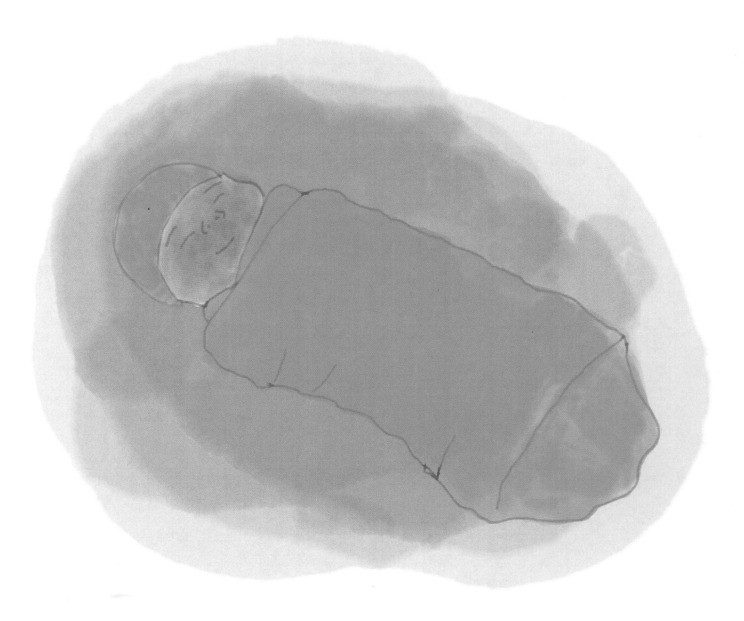

New babies need lots of rest to help their bodies grow big and strong.
Everyone in the NICU needs to use quiet voices so that the babies can
rest.

The doctors and nurses watch the babies carefully. Each baby wears a small red light on his or her foot and stickers on his or her chest that measure the baby's breathing and heartbeat. The doctors and nurses can see the measurements on a computer screen.

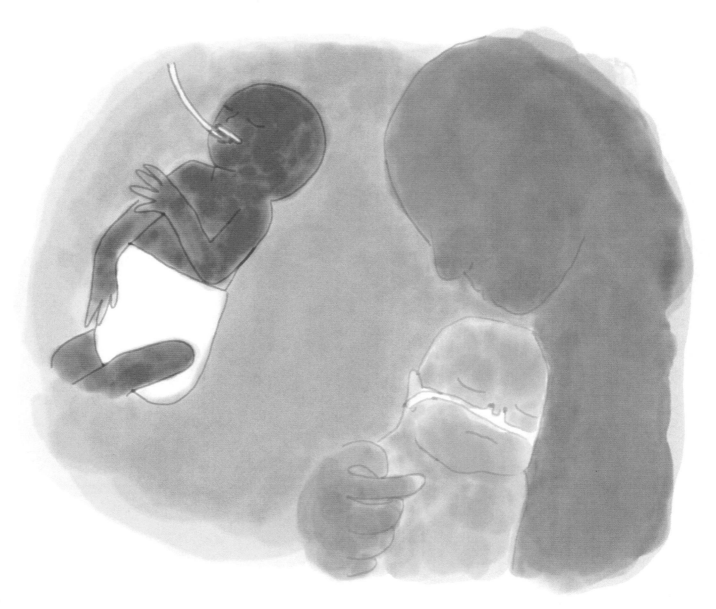

A baby that needs help breathing may have an oxygen tube that rests by his or her nose. If a baby needs more help, the baby may have a breathing tube in his or her mouth. The tube is connected to a machine that breathes for the baby called a ventilator.

Some babies need help learning how to drink milk. If a baby does not drink all of its milk, a nurse can put the rest of the milk in a tiny feeding tube. Feeding tubes go in the baby's nose or mouth and help the milk get to the baby's tummy.

Babies may also have another tube called an IV. The nurses can use an IV to give the baby medicine. An IV can be on a baby's hand, foot, belly button, or head. IVs help the babies get all the medicine that they need.

Babies tell us that they need something by crying. A baby may cry because he or she is tired, hungry, or if something doesn't feel good. If a baby is crying, a nurse, doctor, or parent will check on the baby and help them.

When our baby comes home, our parent will check on the baby when it cries. Crying is okay, but if I don't like it, I can find a quiet place to go and take a break.

Being a new brother or sister, I might have lots of new feelings. I might feel happy that the new baby is finally here. I might feel sad that the baby has to stay at the hospital. Sometimes, I might feel jealous that people are focused on the baby and not me. All of those feelings are okay. I can talk to my family about them.

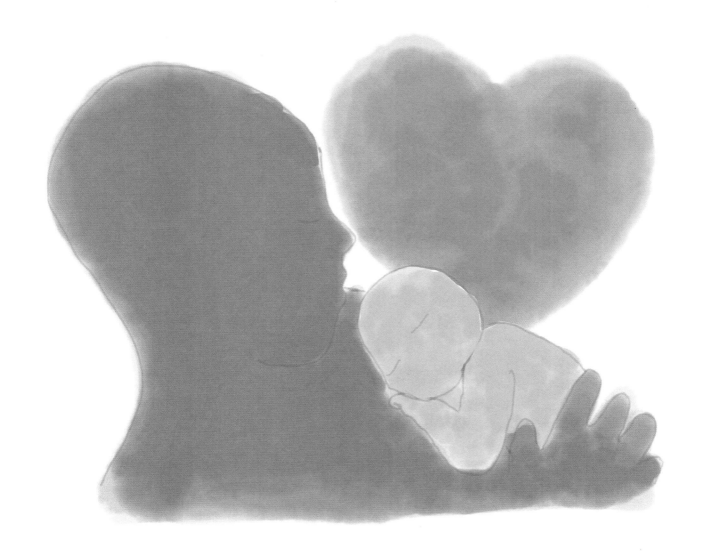

I miss my parent when they are at the hospital taking care of our baby, but when they are there, they are doing a very important job. My parent loves me and our new baby. I know when my parent isn't with me they still love me SO MUCH!

It will feel so good to have my whole family home together. Our baby will be able to come home when our baby is healthy and can drink enough milk to keep growing bigger and stronger. I can't wait for our baby to come home!

When our baby is home, my parent can help me hold our baby. I can help get diapers for the baby and sing to the baby.

I am part of a big team of people who care about our baby! I am a great big _____(brother/sister)!

My picture of our new baby in the NICU.
(Drawing a picture with crayon or colored pencil is a great job for a
new brother or sister! Someday, your baby will love seeing it!)

My picture of our whole family together!

Laura Camerona, Certified Child Life Specialist

With a background in child development, Laura creates books that support children's needs and promote understanding. She specializes in writing books that help parents have hard conversations and support their children during hard times. She loves to partner with passionate people working in non-profit organizations to create books that support families dealing with a variety of struggles.

In a Laura's former career as a hospital Child Life Specialist, she worked in a variety of units, but her last 5 years were spent in the NICU. These families and staff hold a special place in her heart. Laura appreciates the many struggles that come hand and hand with a NICU stay. In this book, Laura focused on finding words that could support families in a large variety of circumstances and illustrations that were representative and inclusive.

Check out Laura's other books and services!

Instagram: @words.worth.repeating
Facebook: @WordsWorthRepeatingBooks
www.wordsworthrepeating.com

Some of Words Worth Repeating's Books:

Words Worth Repeating also collaborates with families to make customized resources.

Does your baby have a new diagnosis? Let's create the perfect resource!

Words Worth Repeating

Words Worth Repeating creates books to promote positive coping and healing for kids and families.

Words Worth Repeating works with organizations and families to create books that give famlies words for hard situations.

Check out the website to learn more!
www.wordsworthrepeating.com